T0148889

Pit to Purpose

God Has Purpose for Your Pain,
a Reason for Your Struggle, and
Reward for Your Faithfulness

Krissy Scott

WESTBOW
PRESS®
A DIVISION OF THOMAS NELSON
& ZONDERVAN

Scripture quotations are taken from the Holy Bible, New Living
Translation, copyright ©1996, 2004, 2015 by Tyndale House
Foundation. Used by permission of Tyndale House Publishers,
Inc., Carol Stream, Illinois 60188. All rights reserved.

WestBow Press books may be ordered through
booksellers or by contacting:

WestBow Press
A Division of Thomas Nelson & Zondervan
1663 Liberty Drive
Bloomington, IN 47403
www.westbowpress.com
1 (866) 928-1240

Because of the dynamic nature of the Internet, any web
addresses or links contained in this book may have changed
since publication and may no longer be valid. The views
expressed in this work are solely those of the author and do
not necessarily reflect the views of the publisher, and the
publisher hereby disclaims any responsibility for them.

Any people depicted in stock imagery provided by
Getty Images are models, and such images are
being used for illustrative purposes only.
Certain stock imagery © Getty Images.

ISBN: 978-1-9736-2284-0 (sc)
ISBN: 978-1-9736-2283-3 (e)

Library of Congress Control Number: 2018903190

Print information available on the last page.

WestBow Press rev. date: 03/19/2018

Testimonials

"I met Krissy Scott one year ago. She is a phenomenal woman after God's own heart. She is like no other woman I have seen in her generation. I had the privilege of hearing her testimony, which is written in this book. Her life could have turned out much different. But because she relies on God and has surrendered her life to Him, He can speak truth in her life and through her life. What impressed me the most was that she never blamed anyone except herself for her actions, which lead to many years of heartache. She rose above the circumstances of her childhood by not accepting the lies of the enemy, repented from her bad decisions, and is now moving forward with God on a journey of freedom and purpose. I am so thankful for a God that saves and extends His grace."

—Janet W.

"No one would have ever imagined that Krissy, the mighty woman of God that she is, would have ever come from such a background as she did. I thank God for the impact she will have on the many lives of women as they read this book and hear her testimony. I thank God for the hope and freedom that each reader will receive from her story. Krissy truly loves God with all her heart, soul, and mind. I am excited to see all of the great things she will be doing for the kingdom."

—Sheila V.

Contents

Testimonials v

Introduction.. xi

Chapter 1 Hope for a Future.................................... 1

Chapter 2 Working Things Together.......................... 9

Chapter 3 A Time Such as This 17

Chapter 4 Finding Hope 23

I call on the **Lord** in my distress,
and he answers me.

Introduction

Thank you for making the decision to read this book. I am a daughter, wife, and mother who has gone through many difficult trials in life. This book is inspired by the Holy Spirit to bring hope, healing, encouragement, and freedom. This is a testimony of specific seasons in my life and how God has carried me through each one. In the pages ahead, you will read about my past mistakes, vulnerabilities, and how God carried me through. I pray that the words you read will sink deep into your heart, where you can find hope and freedom knowing that God is right beside you. He is with you always. He will never leave nor forsake you. There is purpose in your pain. Keep pressing forward no matter what your circumstance looks like. He has a great plan for your life. It's not over for you yet.

"For I know the plans I have for you, says the Lord. They are plans for good and not disaster, to give you a future and a hope."

—Jeremiah 29:11

Chapter 1

Hope for a Future

In the fall of 1981, a daughter was born—not just any daughter, but one who belonged to the Creator of heaven and earth. This child was fearfully and wonderfully made. Every moment of her life was planned out before the foundation of the world was laid. So why would her Creator allow her to live such a difficult childhood? I believe God allows His children to go through trials for our good and His glory. To transform us into His character likeness and to learn we cannot do anything apart from Him.

I was born into a lineage with many generational curses, including alcoholism, drug addiction, abuse, abortion, and many physical ailments. Generational curses are real and exist to take you out! I didn't have any control of who my family would be. I was raised in an environment where alcohol was prevalent. The one who raised me also came from a background of major dysfunction. My mother was a great provider. She worked several jobs not only to provide for our needs but our desires as well. But that came with a high cost as I spent a majority of my childhood with my aunts because my mom worked so much. I remember being dropped off time after time with my aunts and watching my mom drive away. I would cry as I didn't understand why she was gone all the time.

At age five, I was sexually abused by someone I loved and trusted. I lived with shame, confusion, and embarrassment for nearly thirty years before I decided to face the situation head-on. With God's help, I was able to face the abuse by admitting it happened so there could be a time of healing from the violation. Victimesofcrime.org research indicates:

> One in five girls are victims of child sexual abuse. A child who is the victim of prolonged sexual abuse usually develops low self-esteem, feelings of worthlessness, and an abnormal or distorted view of sex. The child may become withdrawn and mistrustful of adults and can become suicidal.

I became that statistic. As years passed, I became suicidal. God is the only way you can heal from such a devastating situation. In my case, He healed and set me free so I can help others heal from their past wounds. I didn't deserve to be violated at the innocent age of five, but it happened. We have the power of the Holy Spirit dwelling inside of us to choose how we will respond to our pasts. Although it took me several years, I finally chose to use my past for God's glory. You can walk in total freedom from the wounds of your past. There is *hope* and *purpose* in your pain.

The void ultimately carried over into her adult life. We moved around a lot growing up. I never felt rooted anywhere we lived because we were never in one location for very long. By the time I was an adolescent, I was bound up in rebellion, harboring resentment, and covered in rejection due to my past hurts and the choices that were made for me in previous years.

The things you allow in your life will affect your children, loved ones, and friends, whether they are negative or positive. You are not the only one affected and suffering. I encourage you to release all things in your life that are not willed by God. I know my mother was the best parent she knew how to be. She has been forgiven. Most parents lead by example on how to become a responsible person. Never underestimate the power of God, as He can take the worst situations and turn them around for good.

My mother taught me a lot through the bad decisions she made. We can still learn the right way to live through bad experiences. It is a *choice* we must make. It would have been easy for me to continue the same lifestyle she lived. By the standards of this world, that should have been the case. But God has a different plan for me to live in freedom from my past and to press on into a life full of purpose toward my destiny.

Reflection Questions

1.   What was your past like?

2.   If your past was difficult and caused hurt, have you forgiven the person(s)?

3.   If your answer is no, what would need to happen for you to give or receive forgiveness?

Prayer Journaling

_____

_____

_____

_____

_____

_____

_____

_____

_____

_____

_____

_____

_____

He is rich in **mercy**.

"We know that God causes everything to work together for the good of those who love God and are called according to his purpose for them."
—Romans 8:28

Chapter 2

Working Things Together

The summer before my freshman year of high school, I found myself having to pick up my life and move to another state. This was the worst news ever! I was just starting to feel comfortable and connected to my surroundings.

Unfortunately, my new living conditions were anything but healthy. Living in this environment pushed me to be become very depressed—to the point of suicide. I begged my mother to let me move back to Indiana to live with family, but it was out of the question. So, one night I decided I was done with life. I took a handful of pills and went to sleep with the intent that my misery would be over. Little did I know at the time that would have been the beginning of eternal torment.

However, my heavenly Father had another plan for me. Exodus 9:16 says, "I have spared you for a purpose—to show you my power and spread my fame throughout the earth." By His grace and mercy,

I woke up in the hospital emergency room once the medical team finished pumping all the medication out of my stomach. You see, the enemy comes to kill, steal, and destroy. He almost took me out for good, and that was his plan. But God intervened and stopped him.

I am alive today because the purpose of my life was ordained before the foundation of the earth was laid. You are reading this book today because there is an ordained purpose for your life. It is not by chance that you are alive. There is no such thing! You were created for a purpose. If you get nothing else out of reading this book, at least allow this truth to saturate your heart and mind. You are worthy of the calling you have been given. You are equipped for the calling you have been given. You are anointed for the calling you have been given. It is not by our own understanding or good deeds but by His will that we are used for His purposes and glory. Once He chose us, He also equipped us for the journey ahead. It is important that you know who you really are in the image of Christ, so you can withstand the struggles of life and the lies of the enemy to come out victorious on the other side.

God says you are:

- A child of God (John 1:12)
- Christ's ambassador (1 Cor. 5:20)
- Completely forgiven (Col. 1:14)
- Tenderly loved by God (Jer. 31:3)
- A temple where God dwells (1 Cor. 3:16)
- Blameless and beyond reproach (Col. 1:22)

- Helped by God (Heb. 4:16)
- Reconciled to God (Rom. 5:11)
- Sanctified (Heb. 2:11)
- A member of Christ's body (1 Cor. 12:27)
- Firmly rooted and built up in Christ (Col. 2:7)
- Born of God so the evil one cannot touch you (1 John 5:18)
- Having needs met by God (Phil. 4:19)
- Given the spirit of power, love, and self-discipline (2 Tim. 1:7)
- A princess in the kingdom of God (John 1:12)
- Assured that all things are working together for good (Rom. 8:28)
- Confident that the good work God has begun will be perfected (Phil. 1:16)
- Chosen by God, holy and dearly loved (Col. 3:12)
- A citizen of heaven (Phil. 3:20)

If you will allow these truths to saturate your heart and mind, you will become unstoppable. The sky will be the limit in what God sends you out to do. It's time for the daughters of the Most High to arise into their purpose.

Are you tired of struggling or going through the motions each day? If we will align our thoughts and actions to the will and Word of God, we will be full of joy and fruitful in all we set out to do. This is God's desire for His daughters. Let's take a stand today. No more days of living in the past. No more days of weariness. No more days of hopelessness. No more days of being beaten down by the lies of the enemy. Today shall be the start of immeasurable joy, limitless faith, and unshakeable trust.

After I was treated at the hospital for the overdose, I was immediately sent to the psychological floor of the hospital for further evaluation. I spent numerous days being watched carefully and attending counseling meetings. The enemy carefully observes our every action. He schemes and lurks while seeking whom he may devour.

Eventually, life went back to usual. As we approached the end of the school year, I received notice from my mom that we were moving back to Indiana. Here we go again: moving. This move was bittersweet as I was happy to be moving back close to family but sad to leave the friendships that I had developed.

I had to start all over again making new friends and getting acclimated with my new life. Being a high school student, moving to a new school is never easy. Friendships have already been developed among people, and outsiders aren't easily welcomed. By God's grace, He helped me establish some good friendships over the next few years.

Still living with rejection, shame, and rebellion, I started dabbling in drugs. Before I knew it, I was selling them. I was bold enough to even sell at school. I was so rebellious that I would do things just to see if I could get away with it. Even through my rebellion, God did not give up on me. Just as He was by my side through my rebellion and disobedience, He is there with you. There is nothing you can do that would make God love you less. He is a forgiving God. He is always full of mercy and love.

Reflection Questions

1.   Do you know what your purpose in life is?

2.   Do you believe God has a plan for you?

3.   If you answered no to the first question, would you like to know?

Prayer Journaling

_____

_____

_____

_____

_____

_____

_____

_____

_____

_____

_____

_____

_____

His **love** endures forever.

"Who knows if perhaps you were
made for a time such as this."
—Esther 4:14

Chapter 3

A Time Such as This

By the time I was a senior in high school, I had been removed from my home, was living on my own, working to pay bills, and going to school to finish my senior year. If that wasn't enough stress, I found myself in an unplanned pregnancy situation. I was so hopeless, ashamed, and scared that I was afraid to tell anyone. I was so bound up in shame that I believed the lies of the enemy. Because I chose to accept the lies of the enemy, I made the decision to terminate the pregnancy. Yes, that's right°... I *chose* abortion. I did not realize the weight that decision would carry for many years to come. I was convinced the problem would go away, and I could move on with my life like nothing ever happened. That is a lie straight from the pit of hell! Life is a gift from God, but it took me a long time to realize that truth.

Abortion affects people differently. Some people will suppress the affects for several years before dealing with them. That is what happened to me. I made the decision and went on with what I thought was a normal life. What I didn't realize at the time was that this decision affected my relationships with other people. I was emotionally unstable and angry much of the time. I had very little patience in all circumstances and would spiral out of control easily. I am not proud of the choice I made; however, I do not dwell there either. I have repented for the choice I made and thank God for His forgiveness.

The healing process began when I realized the weight of my decision and repented. Then, God began His healing work inside me. Over time, I started to notice the healing taking place. I was becoming emotionally stronger, slower to anger, able to keep control of my emotions, and relationships were becoming stronger. As the healing progressed, I began to feel the gentle nudge of the Holy Spirit telling me to step out and share my story with others. This was very difficult to do at first. Unfortunately, we live in a society that tells us we should not talk about our problems or mistakes but instead put on a mask showing the world that our lives are perfect and we don't have troubles. You will know when you are healed because you will be courageous enough to share your story with others. Perhaps this is the moment in which you have been created to share your story for God's glory. Your story may not involve abortion—maybe it is abuse, addiction of some sort, or a marriage that has fallen apart. Whatever your situation is, know that God can turn it around for your good and His glory. He is the miracle maker.

Not even one moment of your past will be wasted when you allow God to move through it. Let Him heal you from the inside out. The real joy will come when you have been freed from the bondage of your past. Freedom came with a very high price—Christ's life. I encourage you to accept this wonderful gift of freedom to move forward from the past so you can live a life of abundance and purpose here on earth and eventually spend eternity with Him.

His **Grace** is sufficient.

"But those who hope in the Lord will renew their strength. They will soar on wings like eagles; they will run and not grow weary, they will walk and not be faint."

—Isaiah 40:31

Chapter 4

Finding Hope

We now fast-forward several years to when I was a twentysomething and met my husband and got married. We encountered two miscarriages, and for the longest time the thought crossed my mind that maybe this was payback for the abortion. I was at a point where I wasn't sure if God would allow me to have children. Those thoughts were contrary to the Word of God, which means on thing—the enemy was lying to me. If you are entertaining thoughts such as this, stop and rebuke them in the name of Jesus! God's love is immeasurable for each of His children and covers a multitude of sins. He desires for me and you to turn from our sin and follow Him by living according to His Word and having an intimate relationship with Him. In 2009, we welcomed a healthy, handsome boy into the world who brings so much joy to our family. Until God gave us a child, I never knew how much you could love another person. The enemy would love nothing more than to torment me with the past abortion and *what ifs* of that situation. You and I cannot dwell in the past. There is no time for us to turn back, dwell in the past, and risk losing the amazing life God has predestined for us. God will meet you right where you are, forgive you, and make your crooked paths straight. He has a great comeback plan for you if you will allow Him to work in you and through you. The opportunity is still there for your life to bloom into something beautiful. I know firsthand as He has taken every broken fragment of my life and is making a beautiful masterpiece for His glory. Be encouraged knowing that you can never mess up so badly that your heavenly Father will leave or forsake you. He is beside you waiting to put together the fragments of your life to make a beautiful masterpiece of you. I hope my story has brought hope as well as encouragement to share your story when He gently nudges your spirit.

God has a **purpose** for your pain, a **reason** for your struggle, and a **reward** for your faithfulness. **Trust** Him.

Reflection Questions

1.   Is there a circumstance from your past that was a heavy burden?

2.   What happened? How did it turn out?

3.   Do you believe that God was alongside you through it all?

Krissy Scott

Prayer Journaling

_____

_____

_____

_____

_____

_____

_____

_____

_____

_____

_____

_____

_____

Additional Journaling

_____

_____

_____

_____

_____

_____

_____

_____

_____

_____

_____

_____

_____

_____

_____

Krissy Scott

Additional Journaling

_____

_____

_____

_____

_____

_____

_____

_____

_____

_____

_____

_____

_____

Additional Journaling

Additional Journaling

Additional Journaling

_____

_____

_____

_____

_____

_____

_____

_____

_____

_____

_____

_____

_____

_____

Krissy Scott

Additional Journaling

Additional Journaling

_____

_____

_____

_____

_____

_____

_____

_____

_____

_____

_____

_____

_____

_____

_____

Additional Journaling

_____

_____

_____

_____

_____

_____

_____

_____

_____

_____

_____

_____

Additional Journaling

_____

_____

_____

_____

_____

_____

_____

_____

_____

_____

_____

_____

_____

_____

_____

Additional Journaling

_____

_____

_____

_____

_____

_____

_____

_____

_____

_____

_____

_____

_____

Additional Journaling

_____

_____

_____

_____

_____

_____

_____

_____

_____

_____

_____

_____

_____

Printed in the United States
By Bookmasters